This Book Belongs To:

____

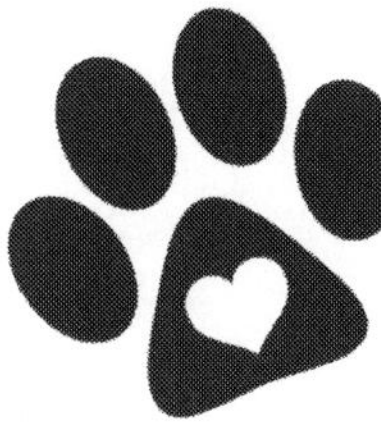

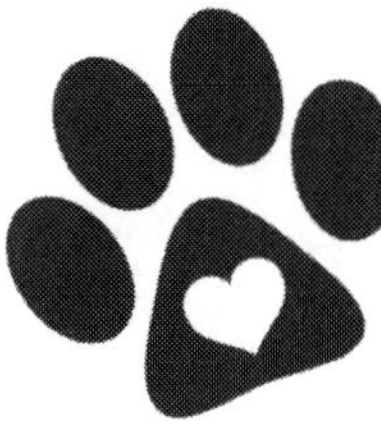

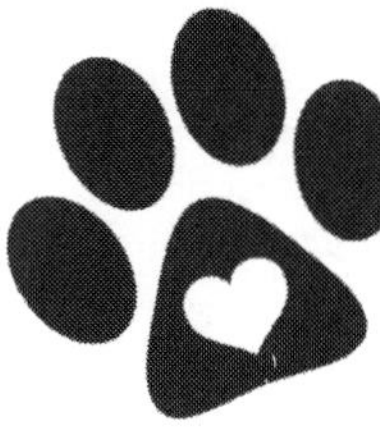

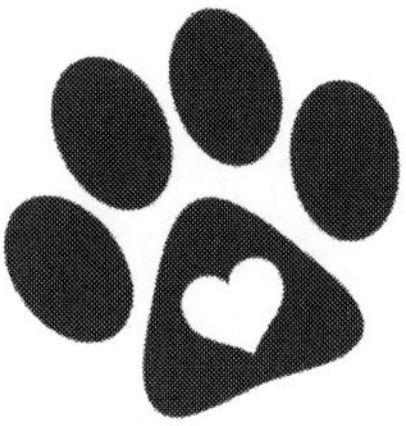

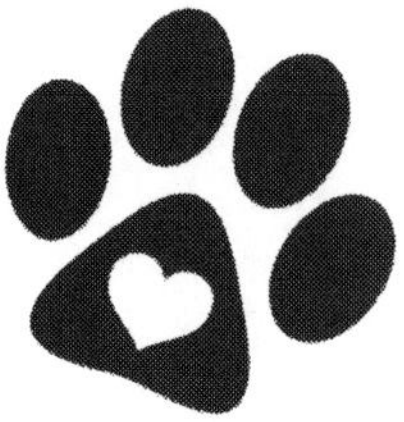

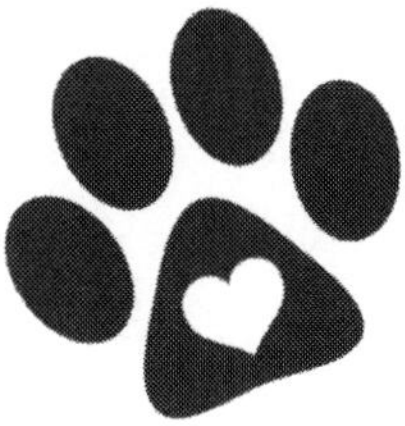

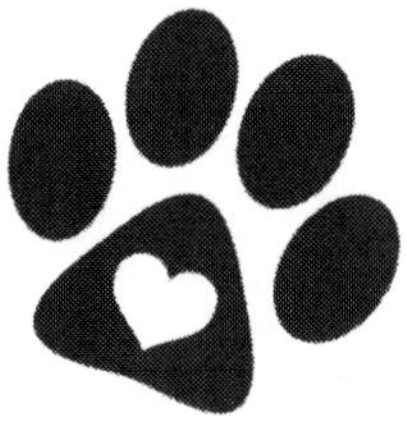

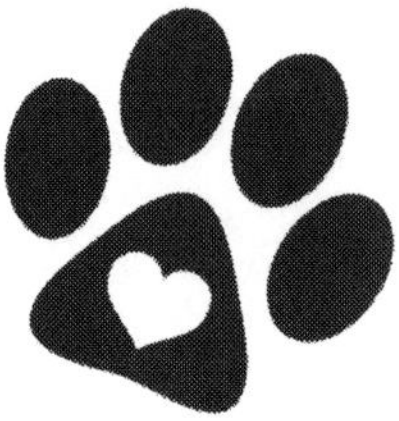

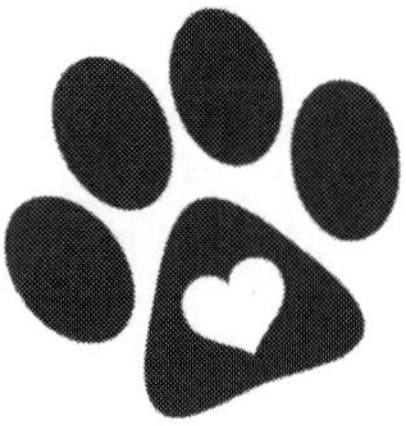

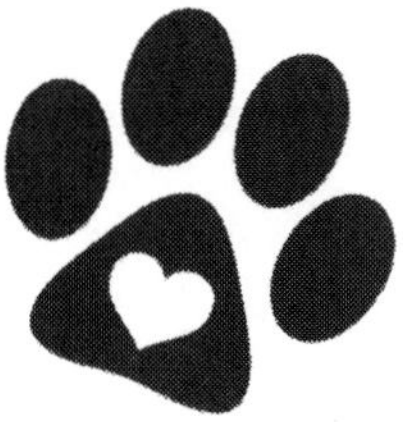

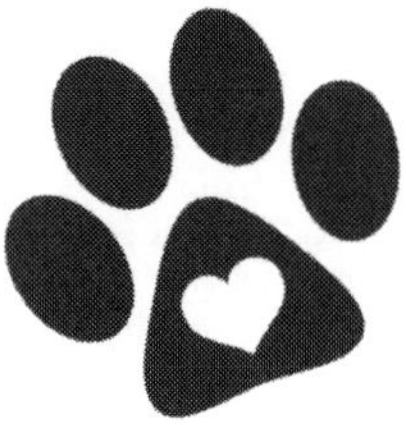

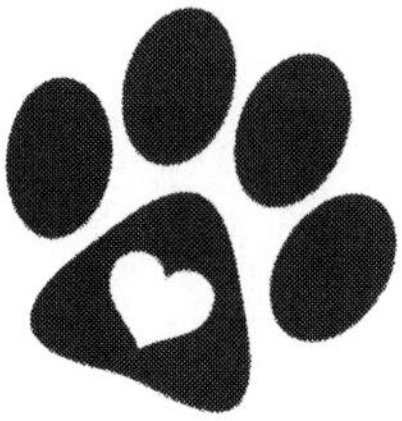

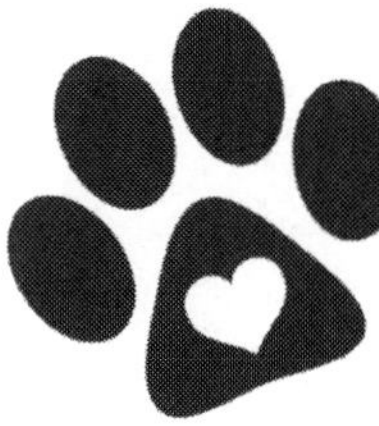

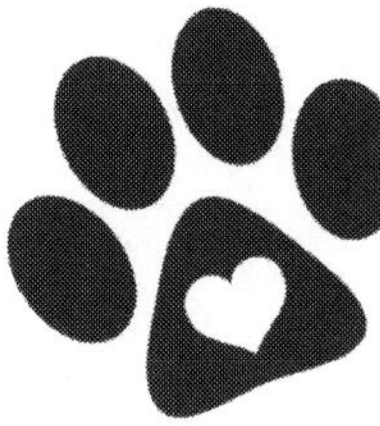

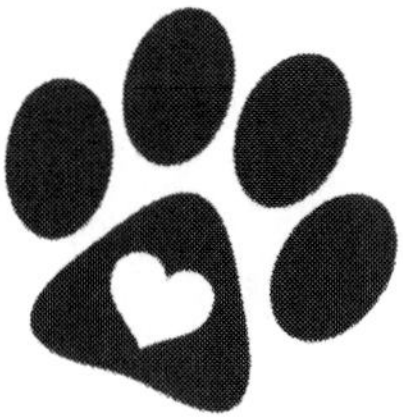

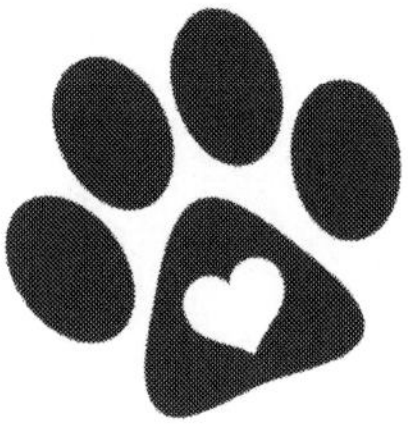

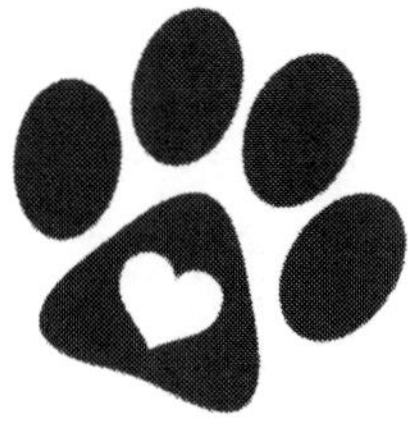

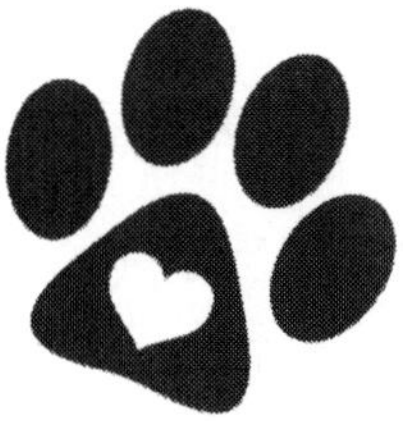

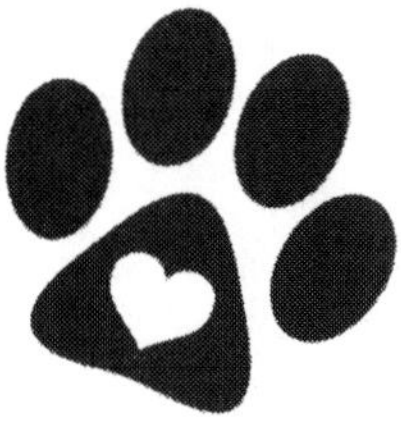

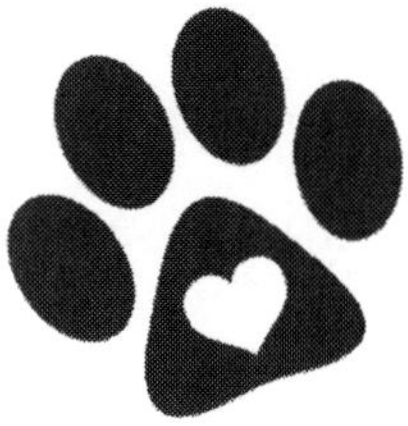

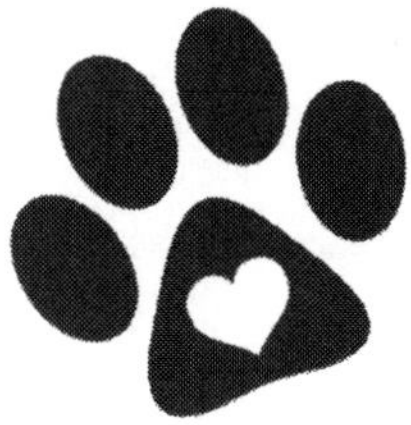

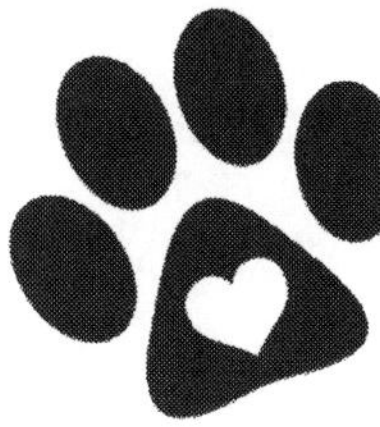

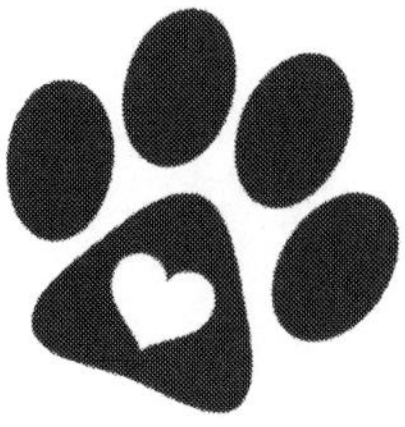

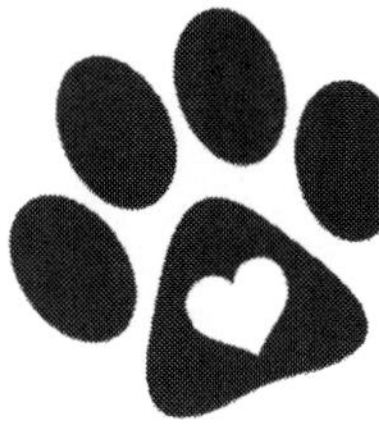

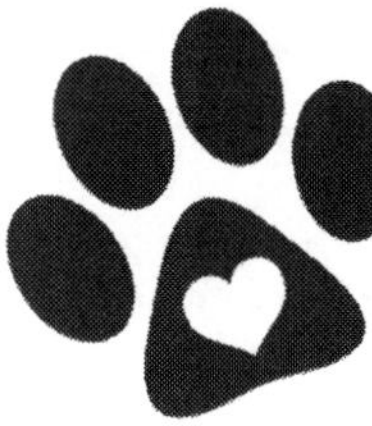

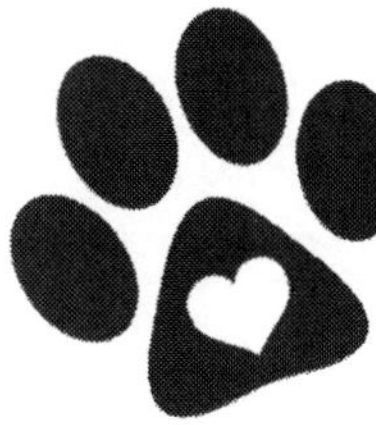

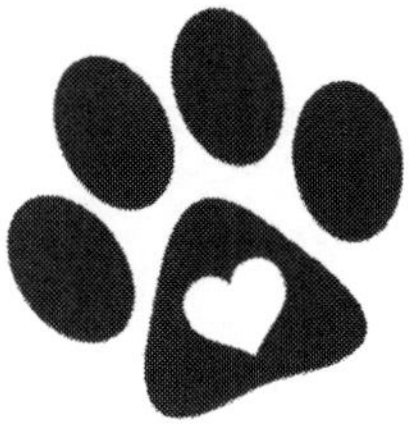

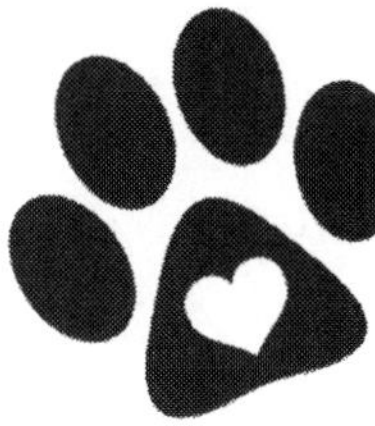

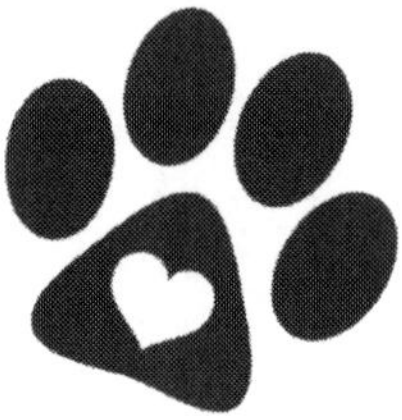

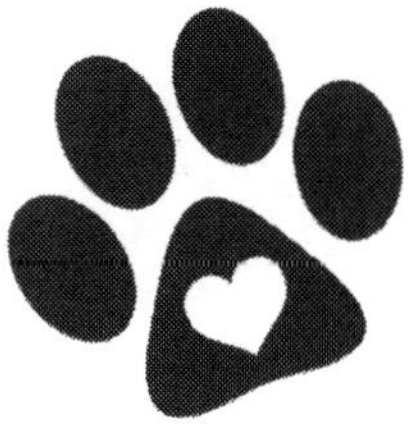

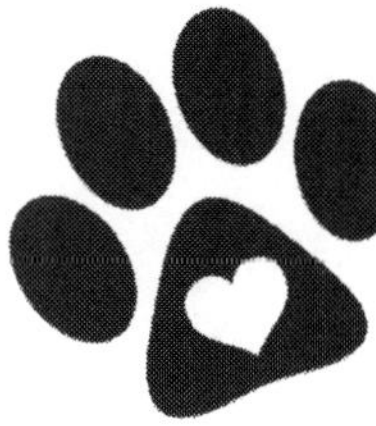

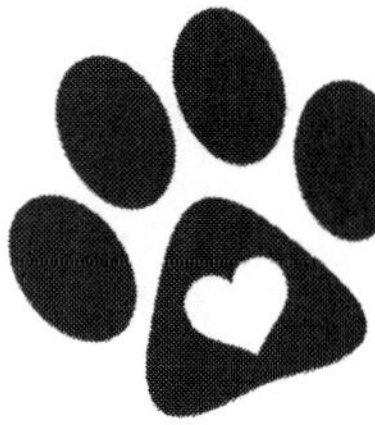

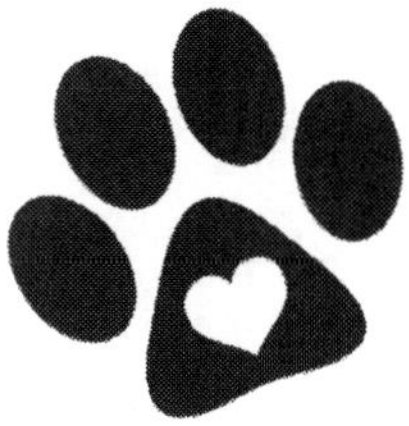

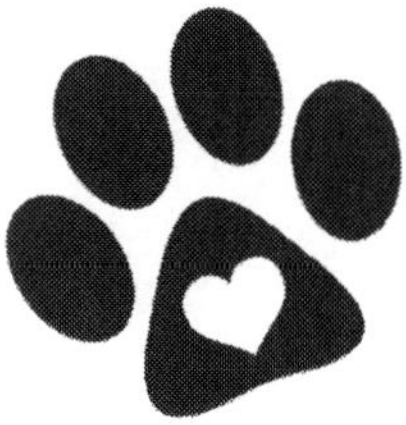

Made in the USA
Coppell, TX
16 December 2021

69018754R00068